# WOOF

## Y York

**BROADWAY PLAY PUBLISHING INC**
224 E 62nd St, NY, NY 10065
www.broadwayplaypub.com
info@broadwayplaypub.com

First printing: May 2012
I S B N: 978-0-88145-527-4

Book design: Marie Donovan
Page make-up: Adobe Indesign
Typeface: Palatino
Printed and bound in the U S A

WOOF was workshopped at the 2010 New Harmony Project with the following cast and creative contributor:

L J FREEMAN ..........................................Samuel Ray Gates
MEL TUDOR..............................................William Salyers
KAREN FREEMAN ...................................Heidi Armbruster
MRS JONES.......................................................... Seret Scott
JACKIE FREEMAN.................................................. Anne Joy
RUBY FREEMAN........................................ Millicent Wright

*Director* ................................................................ Seret Scott


WOOF premiered at Main Street Theater (Rebecca Greene Udden, Executive Artistic Director) on 10 September 2011. The cast and creative contributors were:

L J FREEMAN ..................................................Timothy Eric
MEL TUDOR........................................... Brian H. Thornton
KAREN FREEMAN ............................................ Eva Laporte
MRS JONES.................................. Joyce Anastasia Murray
JACKIE FREEMAN........................................... Maya Wilson
RUBY FREEMAN........................................Alice M Gatling

*Director* ..............................................................Troy Scheid
*Set, props*............................................................ Art Ornelas
*Lighting design* ................................................ Daniel Polk
*Sound design*............................................... Andrew Harper
*Costume design*............................................... Tiffani Fuller
*Production stage manager* ......................... Julie Marie Paré

# CHARACTERS & SETTING:

L J FREEMAN, *30, African American*
KAREN FREEMAN, *30, White American*
JACKIE FREEMAN, *9, their daughter*
RUBY FREEMAN, *45, African American*
MEL TUDOR, *38, White American*
MRS JONES, *58, African American*

*A mid-western American city large enough to have a professional football team. The third millennium.*

*Note: There are no blackouts between scenes. Locations are implied, stuff shouldn't impede, but might accumulate as litter.*

for Chris, Korina, and Kristin Jones

# ACT ONE

## Prologue

*(A large paper poster showing a quarterback throwing a football. It says: "Super Bowl, War of the Titans." Suddenly, bursting through the paper is L J, roaring. He is in street clothes except for a helmet; he carries a football.)*

*(He freezes for a moment, looking like the image in the poster. Then he takes off the helmet, puts down the football as he enters scene one, day two. L J's den. A nervous L J paces, looks out the window. MEL enters with his briefcase.)*

L J: *(Relieved)* Mel, hey.

MEL: Hey, Man.

*(L J embraces him.)*

MEL: I tried to call, I just—

L J: I should have called you—

MEL: It's a circus out there—

L J: How did you get through?

MEL: Curtis made a hole for me. Whatever you pay him, double it. Nobody's getting through Curtis.

L J: Nobody got through Curtis on the line, either.

MEL: I'm...we should— *(Looking in his briefcase)* There's so much—

L J: Sit, sit—

(MEL *takes a yellow legal pad from his briefcase.*)

MEL: ...Are you okay?

L J: Ha—!

MEL: I'm sorry... This can't wait.

L J: What can't wait?

MEL: We need to figure out what you're going to say—

L J: I don't want to say anything.

MEL: People need to see that you're—

L J: Haven't they seen enough?

MEL: They need to see that you're sorry.

L J: I'm sorry, God, I'm sorry.

MEL: Not just about getting caught—

L J: Is that what they think- is that what the idiots think?!

MEL: Hey, it's okay.

L J: *(Over)* It's the truth.

MEL: Good. ...Then it's easier. But the sooner we get out there—

L J: You do it. You say something. You be the spokesman. You do it.

MEL: I can't do it.

L J: What do I pay you for?

MEL: Nobody cares what I say. You have to—

L J: No.

MEL: Okay... We'll wait.

L J: ...How's Rico?

MEL: Furious. Talking to anybody with a microphone.

L J: Oh, man...

MEL: You have to call him.

L J: I'm not calling anybody.

MEL: Okay, okay. We'll just...wait. For a little while.

(*L J takes a drink from a flask.*)

MEL: It's eleven o'clock in the—

L J: Mel. Don't.

MEL: Okay.

(*Brief pause while L J has a drink.*)

MEL: What is that? I've never seen that.

L J: Present from a cop. For an autograph.

MEL: What's in it?

L J: Fancy scotch. He keeps it in this so "nobody knows he's drinking."

MEL: It looks like silver.

L J: They took good care of me. Food, scotch. (*More sarcasm*) Brought me a woman, too. Cops, they know what you need.

MEL: L J—does Karen know?

L J: It was Karen. "We got something for you L J. A real hottie." I wanted to stick my fist down his cop throat. Karen pulled me off. I don't know how she got me outta there. Nobody came with her, a whole locker room full of my teammates and their wives and our friends, and nobody comes. Curtis got me into bed.

MEL: I'm sorry I wasn't there.

L J: I think I'm still drunk—maybe I'm getting drunk all over again.

MEL: I'm not sure how we should play that.

L J: What, play what?

MEL: *(Creatively expositing)* You get caught up in the celebration, the start of the season, last year's Super Bowl winners heading to summer camp to prepare for another glorious season—you have too much to drink you don't know what you're doing. Or you snapped from all the pressure. Temporary insanity.

L J: That's all true. Say all that. What you just said.

MEL: We will pick one explanation. Start piling them on top of each other, it all sounds like a lie. We will pick one truth and stick with it.

L J: Okay, Mel. You pick it. Pick a truth. Pick a truth that will fix it.

MEL: I'll write it, but you have to talk to the press, you're the one has to say it. You have to show—

L J: Fix it before camp.

MEL: There's not enough time—

L J: I want this over.

MEL: It isn't...it doesn't... Oh, God, L J. You're not going to camp.

L J: What—? ...No.

MEL: They dropped you. It's all over the news.

L J: They did not drop me.

MEL: Just give it some time.

L J: They didn't even talk to me.

MEL: Champion saw the tape—

L J: Whatever happened to innocent before proven guilty?

MEL: ...Have you seen the tape?

L J: I don't need to see the tape—I was there.

MEL: It's... *(He stops himself.)* You need to give it some time. It'll blow over— Everything blows over. But not today, not before camp. You might have to sit out the season.

L J: I have a contract.

MEL: There's a clause—

L J: But they still have to pay me—

MEL: No. They have to pay you if you're injured. Morals clause, you're just out. ...Come on, we'll give it some time. America always forgives her heroes. It's the American way.

L J: That's right. I'm a hero. Did everybody forget that?

MEL: You rest for a couple of days, take it easy. I know you didn't...you didn't mean to do it. You were under a lot of stress, and you...snapped.

L J: Yeah, say that.

MEL: I'll work on what you're going to say—for when you're ready. I'll try to get through to Champion.

L J: You haven't talked to him?

MEL: I...I am unable to get past his assistant. But I will. At some point, he has to talk to me. *(Packing up)* I'll call you as soon as I know—

L J: *(Erupting)* I'm sorry, World. I'm sorry Mister Champion. Sorry, sorry, damn fine sorry here—

MEL: I'm doing the best I can, L J.

L J: Call me tomorrow.

MEL: I won't know anything tomorrow.

L J: Call me anyway!

MEL: Okay. I'll go out the back... Are we okay?

L J: Yeah...yes, of course.

MEL: Okay. I'll call you tomorrow. Take care of yourself, L J.

(MEL *exits.* L J *looks out the window, steps back.*)

L J: Karen! Baby?

*(We hear her from afar, then* KAREN *enters.)*

KAREN: What, Honey? Where's Mel?

L J: He left.

KAREN: Oh. Okay. I got to—

L J: Don't go.

KAREN: I'm making—

L J: It can wait.

*(Brief pause)*

KAREN: What were you shouting about?

L J: I'm sorry I shouted.

KAREN: ...I got to feed the kids.

L J: I'll come help you.

KAREN: *(Forcing a smile)* You can't help me feed the baby.

L J: But I can watch.

KAREN: *(Smiling at the much needed joke)* That'll be a big help.

L J: You feed Little L, I'll fix Jackie a sandwich.

KAREN: Really?

L J: Sure, what's the big deal?

KAREN: Nothing. You just— You usually—I thought you'd want to be alone in your den.

L J: Well, I don't.

KAREN: ...The sandwich is made. You can cut the crust off the bread.

L J: Jackie eats the crust.

KAREN: She doesn't like it.

L J: She eats it for me.

KAREN: Because you eat it. She wants to be like you.

L J: What do you do with it?

KAREN: I throw it out. I don't like it either.

L J: Don't do that.

KAREN: Honey, we don't like it.

L J: Give it to me, I like it.

KAREN: I'll give it to the birds.

L J: What birds?

KAREN: The birds...in the yard.

L J: Oh. I thought you went and got her the love birds.

KAREN: I didn't—

L J: Jackie should have the birds. It's good to take care of something. I never got a pet- I had to sneak them in. Frogs. Chipmunks, spiders. Once I sneaked a stray dog up the elevator...God—

KAREN: It's okay—

L J: Big old filthy hound dog. I saved him. I loved him. Ha. Who's going to believe that—? Let's get her the birds—

KAREN: I don't—

L J: We can have what we want. This ain't public housing, we own this house, we can do what we want in our own house.

KAREN: Honey—

L J: We can tear it down, we feel like it. Tear it down, tear it to the ground and shove it up their asses—

KAREN: Shh shh.

L J: What—they gonna take my house away now, my house!

KAREN: It's okay. It's just me.

L J: What?!

KAREN: Shh... It's okay.

L J: I know it's okay, it's my house, it better be okay.

KAREN: Nobody's taking anything. I'm not taking anything.

L J: What do they know, they see the tape, they think they know something, they don't know nothing—

KAREN: We'll get the birds for Christmas...It's not a good idea right now. For us to get a pet.

*(Brief pause. L J quiets himself slightly.)*

L J: Well, you're the boss. You're the boss of the house. We'll wait until Christmas to give my child love birds.

KAREN: ...You drinking that nasty whisky the cop give you? *(She takes it, takes a sip.)* That is awful.

L J: It's very expensive.

KAREN: You want some Coca Cola with it?

L J: Coca Cola and single grain Scotch?

KAREN: Why not?

L J: Not on the Planet Earth.

KAREN: I don't know who makes those rules.

L J: Professional drinking people. So the rest of us don't waste money experimenting. Not to mention the smirks from the frat boys when you order a Coke and Glen Livet.

KAREN: That happen to you?

L J: Don't you know it.

KAREN: Well, I think a Coke would help the burning. Or a glass of ice. Something. *(She takes the flask.)* I'll put this away.

L J: *(Looking around)* Where's my T V?

KAREN: Curtis put it in the garage.

L J: Why? *(Brief pause)* What?

KAREN: I don't want Jackie seeing the tape.

L J: *(Anguish)* Oh no, noooo, I didn't even think, has she—?

KAREN: No, no, it's okay.

L J: I'm her Daddy, she can't see that.

KAREN: I know, she won't—

L J: I gotta— *(He looks out the window.)* Oh man. I gotta—

*(L J grabs his hoodie, and exits out the back. KAREN exits. Scene 2. A school room. MRS JONES peruses her students' drawings. L J enters. The hoodie hides his face.)*

L J: Mrs. Jones?

MRS JONES: Goodness!

L J: Hey, hey—don't be scared. It's just me. Just L J. L J Freeman? Lewis Freeman? *(Removing his hood)* I don't mean no harm.

MRS JONES: My goodness. *(Thrilled)* Mr. Lewis Freeman, is that really you?

L J: Yes, Ma'am.

MRS JONES: You look like one of my gangstas.

L J: I didn't want anybody to know me.

MRS JONES: They sneak in here with the hoodie up so nobody recognizes them. Then they get down on their knees to beg for a D. I don't know why. D's as bad as an F.

L J: A D lets you pass.

MRS JONES: Well, it shouldn't. Goodness, you look so grown. You don't look this grown on the football field.

L J: We're all just a bunch of kids out there. I wasn't sure you'd be here.

MRS JONES: I'm here year round. I tried taking summers off, but I miss the kids too much—even the summer school dummies.

L J: You don't call them that.

MRS JONES: Not to their face. I leave that to their parents. Lewis Freeman. To what do I owe this honor?

L J: Honor? You feel honored?

MRS JONES: Super Bowl M V P? I do, indeed.

L J: I been meaning to come by. Me and Karen moved back when I got traded. It's two years now.

MRS JONES: For goodness sake, I know you live here. I would have to be dead to not know that. I just wondered what brought you by the school.

L J: I was outside- I saw the school...I knew you were still here. From when we were looking for where my daughter should go.

MRS JONES: How old is she?

L J: Jackie's eight. No. She's nine. She's nine now. She's going into fourth grade.

MRS JONES: Do not send her here.

L J: No, we didn't. Karen put her in private school. I wanted her to have you.

MRS JONES: She'll be fine.

L J: A lot of white kids.

MRS JONES: What—? Them white kids too rowdy for your daughter?

L J: She's pretty rowdy herself.

MRS JONES: Just like her Daddy.

L J: She looks like Karen. Both the kids favor Karen.

MRS JONES: The genome is full of surprises...in spite of what Gregor Mendel would have us believe.

L J: See, that's why I want her to have you. She's doing baby work, not genetics.

MRS JONES: She's nine. Nine is habitat and hibernation. That's what you did when you were nine.

L J: I don't remember.

MRS JONES: *(Showing off her memory)* You drew bears in their den.

L J: *(Amazed and remembering)* I did. I drew bears. How do you remember that?

MRS JONES: Mama bear asleep with two baby bears crawling on top of her.

L J: I got an A, no, I got a B+.

MRS JONES: I confess I don't remember your grade.

L J: Closest I'd come to an A. "B+" at the very top of the page so it didn't cover the bears.

MRS JONES: I remember your circuit diagram. We hadn't even done electricity, and you come in with parallel and series all diagramed and explained.

L J: *(Amazed)* I forgot all that.

MRS JONES: I don't remember everybody. I want to be prepared when the reporters come by to interview me.

L J: *(Outburst)* What do you mean?! Who's been here- Don't tell 'em nothin'!

MRS JONES: ...I don't mean anything...You know how the TV people do...when somebody's a star, they interview people who knew him when he wasn't. Like that.

L J: Oh. Yeah. Anybody ever come by?

MRS JONES: No. But I'm prepared if they do. I'll tell them how surprised I was about the football.

L J: You and Mama. I told her I was running track— wasn't even track season- she didn't know. One day, Mister Keeny gives her a free steak. "We gotta keep our L J strong," he says. Busted by the butcher.

MRS JONES: I wasn't surprised that you played. I was surprised you became a professional. I thought you'd be a teacher. Or an engineer.

L J: You thought I'd go to college, even before the football, you thought that?

MRS JONES: I did. You were so curious. "How does it work? How do you put it together?"

L J: I was going to do something with animals. Now I'm a "sports hero." Got nothing to do with animals. *(Brief pause)* Whatchu got them working on?

MRS JONES: *Habitat.* Draw your favorite animal in its habitat. Look at this poor child. Mr. Tommy Abraham has drawn a lion in a cage. What kind of habitat is that?

L J: It's what he knows. Drawing what he knows. Lion in a cage. Looks a little crazy this lion.

MRS JONES: Mister Tommy needs a book on lions in the wild.

L J: You got me a book.

MRS JONES: What was it?

L J: *(Lying)* ...Oh, I guess I don't remember. Mama threw it out cleaning the house.

MRS JONES: *(Remembering)* It was a library book and we had to pay for it. I had to.

L J: *(Serious)* You want I should pay you back now, I can.

MRS JONES: *(Laughs)* Don't worry about it. How is your Mama? She was so pretty.

L J: Still pretty. I bought her a house.

MRS JONES: She used to come on the field trips, bring cookies for the whole class. Nobody does that anymore. She still in the neighborhood?

L J: Oh, no, Ma'am. I got her in a gated community. Meadow Brook.

MRS JONES: Did you see our gates? We're gated, too. To keep us inside. You want to come by? Talk to the kids?

L J: Would they let me?

MRS JONES: What do you mean, "let you?"

L J: Don't you watch T V?

MRS JONES: Not since the Towers.

L J: That's a long time now.

MRS JONES: Mister Jones and I don't miss T V. In season we watch the football, then it's off. I get the Sunday *New York Times* for news. I like to get news late, when the fuss is over. I can't stand the pain of immediacy any more. You know what I mean? *(Brief pause)* You kill somebody, "Assassin?"

L J: *(A laugh bursts)* They don't call me that anymore. How do you know about that? That was high school.

MRS JONES: Me and Mister Jones went to the games. We were fans.

L J: Why didn't you ever say hi?

MRS JONES: You had plenty of fans. You didn't need an old science teacher standing in line to get an autograph.

L J: You wouldn'ta had to wait. Maybe I would have taken up science in college if you had come by.

MRS JONES: What, you got so fancy out there on the football field you forgot about science?

L J: I forgot everything. Football made me feel smart.

MRS JONES: You were smart.

L J: I'm smart when I play. Time stands still, and I think a thousand things in one second, it don't even seem possible how many things I think. A second is as long as an hour.

MRS JONES: I hope science class didn't feel that long.

L J: *(Laughs)* No, I loved it, every hour-long second of it.

MRS JONES: You come by, you talk to the kids. You can tell them about football, long as you tell them how much you love science.

L J: I'm gonna do it. I'm gonna come back and talk to your kids.

(L J *puts his hood back up and exits.* MRS JONES *exits. Scene 3. L J's house.* JACKIE *enters carrying Little L in his carrier.* KAREN *enters.*)

KAREN: Where are you going with your brother?

JACKIE: Outside.

KAREN: You can't take him outside, he's not a toy—

JACKIE: He looks like a toy.

KAREN: Don't you be calling him names.

JACKIE: Pipsqueak.

KAREN: Jackie—

JACKIE: Are you sure he's a boy?

KAREN: You know he's a boy—

JACKIE: Awful little for a boy. Little Little.

KAREN: Your Daddy was little. Then one day he shot up.

JACKIE: He's not going to be like Daddy.

KAREN: Yes, he is, why would you say that?

JACKIE: I'm gonna be like Daddy.

KAREN: You can both be like Daddy.

JACKIE: I'm going to be more like Daddy.

KAREN: Don't you want to be like me?

JACKIE: No. I'm an athlete.

KAREN: You can be an athlete like your Daddy and you can look your Mommy.

JACKIE: I want to look like Daddy.

KAREN: You do, a little.

JACKIE: I look white. Little L looks white.

KAREN: You look light, you don't look white. You get those curls from your Daddy, you're fast like him, you move like him. You're funny like him.

JACKIE: He's not funny.

KAREN: He's just...he's got more responsibilities now. You, me, my parents, Gramma Ruby. And now Little L.

JACKIE: Maybe we should get rid of Little L.

KAREN: He's your brother, he's not a pet—

JACKIE: Does everybody else in your family have blond hair?

KAREN: My family? They're your family, too.

JACKIE: They don't like me.

KAREN: Of course they like you.

JACKIE: I never see them.

KAREN: They're still our family.

JACKIE: They're supposed to be Italian. Italians aren't blond.

KAREN: There's millions of blond Italians.

JACKIE: Not in my school.

KAREN: The Teutons came from the North looking for the sea. Stayed and had babies instead. Blond babies.

JACKIE: I don't know any Teutons.

KAREN: Why are you so cranky? You are pretty and strong and graceful.

JACKIE: I'm not cranky—I'm an athlete. You're the beauty queen. That's why Daddy noticed you.

KAREN: Oh, my friend, you are so misguided.

JACKIE: He fell in love with you when you walked on the beauty queen stage.

KAREN: I didn't do pageants until after we were together.

JACKIE: I saw it on T V. It was a scandal because he was black and you were white.

KAREN: It—it wasn't the dark ages. Your parents are not that old.

JACKIE: It was on T V!

KAREN: We met in the dining hall. The football team ate at one big table. They were scary and loud and mean—

JACKIE: Not Daddy—

KAREN: One day I'm waiting for a chance to sneak by and get my lunch, your Daddy comes over with a plate piled high. "I got you some of everything. I didn't know what you like." That's how we met.

JACKIE: Because you were beautiful!

KAREN: I was not. I was a mouse. But your Daddy had an eye on me. He seemed so grownup even though he was eighteen, same as me. He was from the North, I mean not really North, but everywhere is North to an Alabaman. And black. So it seemed he knew it all.

JACKIE: Why did he notice you if you weren't pretty?

KAREN: I don't know...I was nice. He musta wanted somebody nice.

JACKIE: You're pretty in the yearbook.

KAREN: I made myself pretty for Daddy. It was all for him.

JACKIE: I want to play with Little L.

KAREN: You have to wait for him to ask.

JACKIE: I have to wait until he can talk?

KAREN: Yes. So I can hear when he calls for help.

JACKIE: I'm not going to hurt him.

KAREN: Yes, I think we'll wait until he's bigger than you.

JACKIE: I'll be twenty before he's bigger than me.

KAREN: Okay. You can play with him when you're twenty.

JACKIE: Mom!

KAREN: Okay. Nineteen.

JACKIE: Then give me back the T V.

KAREN: No T V.

JACKIE: Can't watch T V. Can't go to the park. Can't play with Little L.

KAREN: Do a puzzle.

JACKIE: Can I call Lisa and Ariel?

KAREN: I told you no.

JACKIE: Yes, but you didn't tell me why.

KAREN: Honey—

JACKIE: I know Daddy hanged a dog.

(KAREN *is shocked. Brief pause*)

JACKIE: *(Continued)* Everybody knows Daddy hanged a dog.

KAREN: How do you know that?

JACKIE: YouTube. Why was he out on the field?

KAREN: Honey, I don't know.

JACKIE: Ask him. You never ask him anything.

KAREN: He needs to settle for a while.

JACKIE: Where were *you*?

KAREN: Honey—

JACKIE: Why was he so mad? Did you see his face? Mad.

KAREN: I didn't see it. I don't...want to see it.

(JACKIE *makes a horrible face and growls.*)

KAREN: Stop it, stop that.

JACKIE: You should know about it. So you can help.

(*As* JACKIE *describes the scene,* L J *and* MEL *watch YouTube on* MEL's *laptop.* MRS JONES *reads about it in her newspaper.*)

JACKIE: Middle of the field, fifty-yard line. The lights are on like for a game but it's empty except for Daddy. He sits down and he puts his head in his hands. And then Rico's big dog comes up, and she jumps on Daddy's back and starts to lick him in the face, and he grabs her like this and says stuff and his face is all twisted and mean but you can't hear because it's a security camera, not a T V camera. He grabs the choke collar and he holds her up until she's hanged, and his face looks like this—

(JACKIE *makes* L J's *face and snarls loud and long.*)

L J: *(Same time as* JACKIE's *snarl.)* Oh, God, oh my God, God!

(KAREN *envelops* JACKIE *briefly.* L J *hands* MEL *the computer and exits;* MEL *exits.* MRS JONES *exits with her newspaper.*)

JACKIE: He's really strong.

KAREN: Yes, he is.

JACKIE: Why was he crying?

KAREN: I don't know. I told you I don't know. Stop talking about it.

JACKIE: I'm supposed to talk about my problems.

KAREN: This is not your problem!

JACKIE: It is.

(KAREN *takes the baby and exits.* JACKIE *exits. Scene 4.* L J, *agitated, and his mother,* RUBY, *at* RUBY's *house.*)

RUBY: Who's there?

L J: It's me, Mama.

RUBY: Close the door. Close it.

L J: It's closed, I closed it, it's closed. *(As she looks out the window)* What're you looking at?

RUBY: Just checking.

L J: Somebody been by? Reporters been by?

RUBY: What do reporters want with me?

L J: You know how they are—like to know if anything's new. Anybody bothering you like that?

RUBY: Nobody can get through the gate unless they know the password.

L J: Where's the T V?

RUBY: In the other room where it always is. *(He heads toward it.)* You can't watch it.

L J: Why not, what happened?

RUBY: I pulled the wires.

L J: You see something you didn't like?

RUBY: Not since I pulled the wires.

L J: Well, why didja?

RUBY: T V drains me of optimism. I hear those lying men with their crawly names, I just despair. I pulled the wires last winter so I wouldn't be tempted to watch.

*(L J's calming down, figuring* RUBY *hasn't seen the tape.)*

L J: Yeah, there's a lot of lying on T V. So nobody called?

RUBY: No.

L J: *(Relieved)* Good. You let me know you get any phone calls. You don't have to talk to anybody, not unless you know them, or it's me.

RUBY: I keep it turned off.

L J: You keep what turned off?

RUBY: The phone. It's in the drawer.

L J: What if you need to call 911?

RUBY: I'll get it out of the drawer.

L J: Okay. You do that. Just keep it in the drawer.

RUBY: I intend to.... You okay, Lewis? How's my boy?

L J: Sorry, Mama. I guess it's been a while.

RUBY: I don't need to see you long as I get to see my Jackie. Every other Tuesday they take Gramma Ruby to Ruby Tuesday's.

L J: That's funny.

RUBY: I know; it was my idea. The last few weeks it's just been me and Jackie. When is your wife gonna bring me my grandson?

L J: He's too little for a restaurant.

RUBY: I hope I see him before he enters college.

L J: Mama...you'll see him.

RUBY: I'm just saying. ...How's the season coming?

L J: Season was over four months ago. Don't y'all talk about the games?

RUBY: We talk girl talk.

L J: I win the Super Bowl, Jackie don't see fit to mention it?

RUBY: Must have slipped her mind with the excitement of visiting me. Congratulations, Mister Q B.

L J: I said hello to you. "I'd like to say Hi to my Moms."

RUBY: Well, Hi back, and this is a much nicer greeting than through the T V wires.

L J: How would you know? You didn't see it.... Yard's looking kind of raggedy.

RUBY: I got it under control.

L J: Don't look under control to me. Looks like the yard guys been neglecting you for some time.

RUBY: Well. If you must know...I told them not to come anymore.

L J: That's fine, who needs yard guys. I'll come by and cut your grass. You don't need no yard guys bothering you.

RUBY: No need for anybody to be cutting anything. I'm creating a habitat for birds and small mammals. Birds and small mammals like it raggedy.

L J: The Association rules say—

RUBY: Those people are unreasonable.

L J: They're just worried about their property values.

RUBY: They don't even know I'm here.

L J: They know you're here.... Did you fire the housekeeper? Smells funny.

RUBY: Well. It just needs a good airing out.

L J: You fired the housekeeper.

RUBY: We didn't see eye to eye about some of the bedrooms. And she had a tendency to overuse chlorine bleach. That is very bad for the water.

L J: Karen know you fired the housekeeper?

RUBY: Don't blame Karen. I wait for Karen and Jackie at the gate— Soon as you invite somebody inside it's all "what's that smell?" and "who's mowing the grass?"

L J: Okay, Mama, I get it.

RUBY: You want something? A sandwich? I still got that brandy Mel gave me three years ago.

L J: No. No brandy. I'm off all that. Never again.

RUBY: ...What's going on with you, Lewis? Tell me.

L J: Nothing, nothing's going on...

RUBY: Something is going on.

L J: (*Thinks something up*) ...Okay, there is. I got me another Daddy.

RUBY: How many is that?

L J: Three. Three men are now L J Freeman's Daddy.

RUBY: Put your phone in the drawer, you won't get any more Daddy calls.

L J: You could help me out with this, Mama.

RUBY: There's no help for it. I was a silly girl. I got myself in trouble with one boy, not three.

L J: A boy named Roger.

RUBY: Yes.

L J: They're all three named Roger.

RUBY: Baby, why you bothering me with this?

L J: I ain't bothering you—you asked me what was going on.

RUBY: I told you to pick the one you want. Pick the nicest. The one who is nicest to you. Say, "you are nice and you are my Daddy, goodbye Other Two Fake Daddies, go away, Other Two Fake Daddies."

L J: None of them are nice. All my Daddies show up with their hand out.

RUBY: If it's so important to you, make them take a test. Don't they give a test for that now?

L J: How long would it be before that was on T V?

RUBY: Pull the wires. Then you won't know.

L J: How can a man up and leave his child? First time I held Jackie, a flood rushed into me, almost knocked me down. Same thing with Little L. A flood. I could never turn my back on them.

RUBY: In the first place, your Daddy wasn't no man. He was a boy. Second place, he never saw you. If he'da saw you, he wouldn't have left you. You were impossible to leave. If it was possible I'da left you myself—you were a lot of trouble.

L J: L J Freeman does not know who his Daddy is. Don't make you look good, neither.

RUBY: Why? What's that got to do with me?

L J: *(Can't help but laugh)* Never mind. It's all right.
Don't worry about any of them Rogers. We got Curtis
to take care of our Roger problems.

RUBY: You're the one brought it up. I wasn't worried at
all before you brought it up. Seems to me the important
thing is that you *be* a Daddy, not that you get to get
one. Thirty years old, wants a Daddy.

L J: Okay, okay. I'm a Daddy, okay?

RUBY: Most important thing you are.

L J: I said okay.

RUBY: You a good man, L J Freeman.

L J: Why?

RUBY: Cause you never up and left a poor girl gonna
have a baby.

L J: Don't be so sure. Maybe there's little L J's all across
America.

RUBY: Tell me that's not so. You tell me.

L J: It's not so. You had me scared to death to even look
at a girl.

RUBY: Didn't hurt you none to wait. *(Brief pause)* Little
thrush woodies got some eggs laid in a tree out there.
You want to see?

L J: Some other time. ...Mama? If I sell this house, are
you alright with that?

RUBY: No, that is not alright. Why would you think
that is alright?

L J: Apartment might be better. People closer, looking
in on you, some friends.

RUBY: I don't like to move.

L J: You don't like it here. People aren't friendly.

RUBY: I'm just getting it right. A habitat for small mammals and birds where once was a water-greedy lawn.

L J: If you make your habitat, I guarantee the Association will be all over it.

RUBY: I am invisible to them. No one comes by. No one waves from their dark car.

L J: ...We could sell my house—move in here. My house is the one with the mortgage. Mel said take a big mortgage and put the cash in the stock market where it would make me rich. Ha.

RUBY: You bring your family on over. I will make them a habitat.

(L J *exits. Scene 5. Day three.* MEL's *place.* KAREN *and* MEL.)

KAREN: Know him? You think I know him? Because I'm married to him? You don't get to know somebody because you're married to him. Who you get to know is yourself, your petty pathetic needy little self. You don't know him. And then one day it all explodes and everybody is asking you how did it happen and why didn't you stop it and where were you? And you have nothing nothing to battle them off with because everything that you had is simply gone—

MEL: Come here—

KAREN: Why is everybody so surprised, so astonished? All the hypocrites are astonished! They pay him to be an animal and they are astonished when he is one. Do you know what it's like after a game, he comes home after a game? He's like a bomb going to explode. I am so careful, so quiet, so deliberate. Until he realizes the game is over, and no one in our house wants to hurt him. His ridiculous generosity to anybody who asks for anything, even when it's a bald out lie, that's so he can tell himself he's a person. He's not an animal, he's a person.

MEL: You're upset.

KAREN: Upset? I'm upset?

MEL: Why did you come if you won't let me comfort you—?

KAREN: Did you tell him?!

MEL: *(brief pause)* No. That's up to you, that's always been up to you.

KAREN: I thought you told him—I thought that's why he—

MEL: I didn't.

KAREN: Well, don't. Don't tell him, don't ever tell him. That's all he needs. I thought it was fine, I thought we were fine. How could he do this? Where did this come from?

MEL: Please stop talking to me about your husband.

KAREN: Who am I supposed to talk to?

MEL: Karen...I haven't seen you...

KAREN: You've seen me.

MEL: I haven't...seen you. I don't know who you want me to be.

KAREN: I want you to be L J's friend.

MEL: I'm not his friend. I'm your friend. I'm his lawyer.

KAREN: I don't know what to do. I can hold it together for L J and Jackie, but Little L? Babies know. You pick up a baby, they know, they start to cry. You have to be relaxed, happy. Little L cries when I pick him up.

MEL: I saw him.

KAREN: Who?

MEL: Little L. I saw him yesterday. I never saw him before.

KAREN: Yes, you did.

MEL: No. He's always "asleep", even though I can hear him. He's asleep when I come by. Curtis has him at the park when I come by.

KAREN: He's a baby. He looks like a baby. *(Pause)* What?

MEL: I did always wonder.

KAREN: You didn't wonder enough to ask!

MEL: *(Rhetorical)* Why did you come to me?

KAREN: To find out if you told him—

MEL: It's why you came to me in the first place.

KAREN: I came to you...because I was losing him, I could feel him slipping away and I was lost. I'm not losing him now, he needs me now.

MEL: What do you need?

KAREN: Don't do this.

MEL: Someone to talk to, someone who listens, a reasonable person, to relax, to be yourself. You need to be with your people.

KAREN: Stop it, you're ridiculous. L J is my people.

MEL: Doesn't he wonder? When he looks at Little L?

KAREN: *(Overly defensive)* Wonder what? Jackie's light—Little L is light—L J and I have light children, so what?

MEL: *(Can't believe it)* Oh, Karen...What about me? Don't I have some rights?

KAREN: You have no rights. You are an interloper.

*(KAREN exits. MEL exits. Scene 6. The school. MRS JONES and L J. L J sits at a child's desk. She is withdrawn, angry.)*

L J: I was trying not to scare the kids—

MRS JONES: Big hulking man in a hoodie sneaking into the school. You scared them.

L J: You told me to come talk to them!

MRS JONES: Then call and make an appointment— Get rid of that sweatshirt. You look like a hoodlum. You need a shave.

L J: I spent the night at Mama's. The yard guys dropped me here—Mama is friends with all the yard guys—she don't know her neighbors, but she knows their yard guys— "Where you like go, Señor Freeman?"

MRS JONES: Get up from that desk—you're going to break it.

*(Pause. L J looks at MRS JONES. She looks away.)*

L J: You saw it.

MRS JONES: I didn't see it, I'm not going to see it, I could never look at that. I read about it. Mr. Jones saw it.

L J: It's worse when you look at it. It's way worse. It's so worse, you can't imagine how worse.

MRS JONES: Get up from there. ...Come on. Get up. You can help me move the desks. We have report circle tomorrow.

*(L J stands but does not move the desk.)*

L J: Summer kids do reports?

MRS JONES: Of course they do. I don't want to cheat the dummies out of the full Mrs Jones experience. Don't just stand there, help me.

L J: I can't.

MRS JONES: *(Sarcasm)* Your contract don't allow it?

L J: *(Agitated)* I can't lift a desk, I can't even tie my shoes. I can't do anything—

MRS JONES: *(Over)* What are you—

L J: *(Over)* I don't know what to do. There's no place I can go. I ride around with yard guys. "Where we take you, Señor Freeman?" The only people talking to me are talking Spanish—

MRS JONES: Settle down, now.

L J: It wasn't a dog jumped on my back, it wasn't a big ol' dog, it was a Detroit Lion. Champion showed game films at the party, he thought it would be funny—a whole reel of me getting knocked on my ass. And there it is right in the middle of the funny film—the end of a nothing game, we're up three touchdowns, why am I still playing? Why am I still throwing passes? I drop back to pass, and my offensive line, the most unbreakable line in the N F L—breaks, and a three hundred pound Detroit Lion flattens me. Pain—fire—his helmet in my back. The pain doesn't go away. I go to Dr Scott cause I know he ain't gonna tell, he ain't gonna call the newspapers. He shoots me up so I can play. But the pain doesn't go away. I play a whole season with fire in my back—but I throw, I always throw— It's me gets us to the Super Bowl. The last drive of the biggest game of my life, my arm freezes, and I call draw plays— "I'm a genius, I fool the defense" that's what everybody says—but I'm only handing off because my arm don't go forward!

MRS JONES: Keep your voice down.

L J: *(Over)* It don't go. All spring I'm sneaking to the east side getting shot up with who knows what, but it don't go forward. And I'm supposed to start training camp—that's why they're having this party— everybody's there—all the gimme people, everybody with his hand in my pocket, helping me "celebrate" a new start. I'm the best quarterback in the league, except my arm don't go forward.

MRS JONES: Then get out of the game.

L J: How am I supposed to live without football? There's no money, there's nothing. The only way I have enough money is if I die.

MRS JONES: ...Retired football players rarely starve, Lewis.

L J: I didn't mean to hurt anything. I left the party so I wouldn't hurt anything. Everybody laughing at me and sucking up to me, and that dog, that big old sweet dog jumps on me and I'm back in Detroit, and the pain, "You will not do this to me, you dog, you will not, you will not!" (*The fierceness fades. He catches his breath.*) Then they're all there, and I'm screaming and Rico's crying. He gets the security tapes to the T V station before the sun comes up.

MRS JONES: This is not Rico's fault.

L J: I didn't say it was.

MRS JONES: I don't know what you expect of me—you do something against everything I believe, against everything I ever taught you. You sit there in your gangsta hoodie. What do you want?

L J: I want...I want...

(MRS JONES *turns away.* L J *exits. Scene 7.* RUBY *and* JACKIE *at* RUBY'S. *Binoculars*)

JACKIE: What's the little red one?

RUBY: That is a red thrushed woodie.

JACKIE: What's the yellow one?

RUBY: That is a yellow thrushed woodie.

JACKIE: What's the little brown one with the black on his face?

RUBY: That is a brown thrushed woodie with black eye.

JACKIE: Where'd you learn so much about birds, Gramma?

RUBY: We had birds in the apartment. Used to put seeds on the window ledge, birds had a regular party.

JACKIE: Sure are a lot of them.

RUBY: They all love that feed mix. Plus cornbread.

JACKIE: That's cornbread in the birdfeeder?

RUBY: With extra butter. Fat for the winter.

JACKIE: It's summer, Gramma.

RUBY: They bulk up over the warm months. I'm going to put out the big pot so they can have a bath.

JACKIE: Get them a birdbath.

RUBY: Why? I got me that good pot. I don't need it anymore for cooking. Nobody comes by.

JACKIE: I come by.

RUBY: Yes, but that pot is for a crowd. Hasn't ever been a crowd come by to this house for a meal.

JACKIE: We have a birdbath.

RUBY: Birds use it much?

JACKIE: It don't get filled unless it rains.

RUBY: Use the hose. Fill it up for the birds.

JACKIE: I'm going to send them over here to take a bath in your big pot. ...Something is in the bushes.

RUBY: Probably squirrels. They eat what falls. I grease the pole.

JACKIE: Why?

RUBY: Squirrels don't like to get their paws all nasty. So they don't climb up it anymore. They were running off all the little thrush woodies.

JACKIE: Looks like Sleeping Beauty's bramble patch out there.

RUBY: Nobody gets in and nobody gets out. Not for a hundred years.

JACKIE: How we supposed to eat?

RUBY: We will live off the land. We are hunter-gatherers.

JACKIE: You're a card, Gramma. Can we watch T V?

RUBY: I yanked the wires.

JACKIE: How do you watch Daddy?

RUBY: Oh, Baby, I can't watch those games. All those big men chasing Lewis. Breaks my heart.

JACKIE: Daddy is tough.

RUBY: He's not that tough.

JACKIE: You got wireless?

RUBY: Oh, probably, I got everything. What is it?

JACKIE: It's for computers.

RUBY: I don't have those.

JACKIE: I need to show you something on YouTube.

RUBY: We'll just watch our birds.

JACKIE: I want love birds, but Mommy says they're messy.

RUBY: You don't want to keep birds in no cage. Get yourself a feeder and some cornbread.

JACKIE: Let's play with Esmeralda and Miss Patch.

RUBY: Are those the two young ladies come over with you?

JACKIE: *(Gets her dolls)* Gramma, I'd like you to meet Esmeralda and Miss Patch.

RUBY: How do you do, Ladies. I'll be the patchy one.

JACKIE: No. You're pretty. You be Esmeralda.

RUBY: All my dolls were white. I never saw the black dolls until I was too old to play.

JACKIE: Everybody gives me black dolls.

RUBY: Oh, they mean well. They're just afraid they're gonna make a mistake.

JACKIE: I like black dolls.

RUBY: I'll get you a pretty white doll looks like your Mama. These two girls get along?

JACKIE: They do whatever we make them do. *(As Miss Patch)* "Where you going all dressed up like that, Miss Esmeralda?"

RUBY/ESMERALDA: "To the Moon, Miss Patch."

JACKIE/MISS PATCH: "I never heard of somebody going to the Moon."

RUBY/ESMERALDA: "Got a great view from up the Moon."

JACKIE/MISS PATCH: "It's too far away, the moon, for a view. What do you think you'll see?"

RUBY/ESMERALDA: "I will see Nothin'!"

JACKIE/MISS PATCH: *(Astonished)* "You going all that far to see a view of Nothing?"

RUBY/ESMERALDA: "Sears Tower, Eiffel Tower, Leaning Tower of Pisa, Twin Towers, they are nothin' on the Moon. That's what I want to see. All the big things be nothing to the Moon."

JACKIE/MISS PATCH: "Well, I'm sorry I even asked. Did you see L J Freeman on the T V?"

RUBY/ESMERALDA: "No T V here."

JACKIE/MISS PATCH: "It's all over the T V and the YouTube what he done." *(brief pause, then, urgent, as herself.)* Ask me what he did. Ask me.

RUBY: Give me that Patchy gossip. *(To the dolls)* How many times have I told you never to gossip? Gossip is mean and don't do the world a lick of good. Don't you be speaking ill of Jackie's Daddy. Man is the most giving man in the universe. I'm setting you two girls in your room as punishment. *(She exits with the dolls.)*

JACKIE: ...I'm sorry—I won't gossip any more, I promise. ...Gramma?

*(JACKIE exits. Scene 8. L J's house. Little L in his carrier. L J looks inside.)*

L J: What are you looking at? Go back to sleep. ...What's so funny? Don't you know who you're laughing at? Jessie James, Sadaam Hussein, gunslinger, murderer, terrorist. What? You don't care? You *don't* care, look at you. Handsome little guy. Look just like your Mama. Hee hee, yeah, your Daddy's a comedian. *(He puts his hand in the carrier.)* That is one pitiful fist. How you supposed to catch a football with that? We won't tell your Mama. If it's up to her, you'll never play ball. She thinks you'll get a scratch, it'll get infected, you'll go to the hospital, you'll lose a leg. Your Mama at the beach? Wouldn't go in the most beautiful warmest ocean. Too scared of what's underneath.

*(JACKIE enters.)*

JACKIE: Why's he so white?

L J: He'll come into his color. You did.

JACKIE: When?

L J: ...Soon... Should be soon now... Where you been?

JACKIE: Gramma's. Curtis brought me. Where were you last night?

L J: Gramma's.

JACKIE: *(She laughs.)* What were you telling him?

L J: Not to be scared.

JACKIE: He don't have nothing to be scared of, he's not in school. School's where all the meanies are.

L J: What meanies?

JACKIE: There's plenty of 'em. I deal with shit every day.

L J: Don't say shit.

JACKIE: You do.

L J: I'm thirty. You can say shit when you're thirty. Come here.

*(JACKIE jumps into L J's arms.)*

L J: *(Pain)* Oh, man, oh man. *(He lets her down.)*

JACKIE: I'm not that heavy.

L J: *(Trying to recover.)* Yeah, you packing it on. You eating like Curtis.

JACKIE: I told them Curtis is my bodyguard.

L J: Who you tell that to?

JACKIE: The meanies. I said he's got a gun. I made Kallie cry and pee her pants.

L J: Jackie—

JACKIE: She deserved it. I should have smacked her.

L J: You don't smack.

JACKIE: All last year, *(Sings)* "Who's your Daddy? Who's your Daddy? Who's your Daddy? Jackie Jackie, who's your Daddy?"

L J: That don't mean nothing.

JACKIE: She says "I'm blacker than you and I'm white."

L J: You tell her the genome is full of surprises.

JACKIE: I told her I spit in her sandwich.

L J: Did you?

JACKIE: I would have if I coulda got it. She cried.

L J: The other kids the ones need the bodyguard.

JACKIE: Yeah. Can I pick him up?

L J: What's Mama say?

JACKIE: She says yeah.

L J: No she don't.

JACKIE: How do you know?

L J: 'Cause you can't lie for squat. Whachu studying in school?

JACKIE: It's summer vacation.

L J: What did you learn in science?

JACKIE: Wetlands, drylands, lowlands, highlands, midlands, tundra lands and step lands. I had fractions.

L J: I don't think I had fractions in fourth grade.

JACKIE: Third. Fourth is next year.

L J: I know I didn't have them in third grade.

JACKIE: You were in public school. They're crap.

L J: Don't talk like that.

JACKIE: That's what you said. "I don't want her in public school, they're crap." Can I have a cell phone?

L J: What does Mommy say?

JACKIE: She says yes.

L J: I know that's a lie. You can use the telephone. You don't need a cell phone.

JACKIE: The telephone doesn't take pictures.

L J: You have a camera.

JACKIE: The camera doesn't text.

L J: You can do email.

JACKIE: Email is slow. What if I need to talk to someone and it's dinner and it's night?

L J: You wait until tomorrow.

JACKIE: Lisa and Ariel have cell phones that get email.

L J: No.

JACKIE: Teach me football.

L J: You know football.

JACKIE: Not the rules. How to play.

L J: Girls don't play.

JACKIE: In the future they will. Little L is just about the right size.

L J: In about sixteen years.

JACKIE: I don't mean "to play." I mean "to throw."

L J: *(Picking up Little L.)* This ball would wobble even more than a regulation one.

*(Which makes JACKIE very happy. Enter KAREN and MEL who carries a box of trophies, which he puts down.)*

KAREN: What are you doing, Honey?

L J: I was...

JACKIE: *(Over, she has put on L J's helmet.)* Daddy's going to pass me Little L like a football—now, Daddy!

KAREN: L J!

MEL: *(Same time)* No!

*(Brief pause. L J is dismayed.)*

L J: We're just playing, Baby.

JACKIE: Come on, Daddy. Toss me Little L.

L J: *(Sarcasm)* Ordinarily I would. But seeing as how your Mama gets so upset, we'll wait 'til she's not around.

KAREN: L J—

MEL: He's having us on, Karen... Let's have a look at that football. *(He takes the baby.)* Hey there, Son. Some day we're going to tell you the story of your first football game when you were the ball, and L J Freeman ran you home for a touchdown.

JACKIE: You don't think he'll get bigger than me, do you?

MEL: I do, I think he will outgrow us all.

KAREN: Give him to me—he's wet.

MEL: How can you tell from over there?

KAREN: I can...just tell, and he's due to be wet, here.

*(L J has noticed the snippy exchange. KAREN takes the baby. MEL looks adoringly at the child. L J circles completely around the couple, reeling, as he considers Little L's parentage for the first time. JACKIE watches him until:)*

JACKIE: Woof! *(She has their attention.)* Woof!

*(The adults look at her. She produces a dog's choke collar.)*

JACKIE: This was on the door with a note. "L J Freeman. You lynched the wrong dog."

### END OF ACT ONE

# ACT TWO

*(Scene 1. L J's house. Day five.* KAREN *and* L J. *Packing boxes.* L J *studies Little L in his carrier.)*

KAREN: L J, are you going to help or not?

L J: I helped. I made the decision.

KAREN: You make the decision, and I pack the house?

L J: Well. I made the decision. That's something.

KAREN: L J!

L J: I'm not any good at it. All those dishes that came smashed when we moved here?

KAREN: You didn't wrap them. You just put them in the box.

L J: That's what I'm saying. You wrap good.

KAREN: If you're not going to pack, go study your speech.

L J: I looked at it.

KAREN: Can you say it by heart? Mel says it's better if you don't have to read it.

L J: Oh, he does, huh?

KAREN: Yes, he does. What is wrong with you?

L J: ...I know the speech.

KAREN: Let me hear it.

L J: I'm not going to practice it to you.

KAREN: I want to hear how it sounds.

L J: You can hear it when everybody else hears it.

*(Brief pause)*

KAREN: You're going to wake him up.

L J: He sleeps through the storm. Wouldn't you like to be him? Eat, drink, laugh, cry, sleep. Hold tight to L J's finger. Smile a know-nothing sleeping smile. So happy. You have to love that happy little smile.

KAREN: You're making me nervous standing there.

L J: Whatchu got to be nervous about?

KAREN: Oh, I don't know—I'm selling my house at a loss; my husband lost his job, and we're moving in with his crazy mother—

L J: You don't like it when I call her that.

KAREN: I didn't mean to. I'm sorry— You say it in front of Jackie. I don't want her to hear that. I'm just nervous.

L J: Look at your peaceful son. Takes all my nerves right out of my body.

KAREN: Somebody has to pack. Everybody stands around looking at Little L, nothing's going to get done.

*(Baby wakes up.)*

L J: There you are. *(Urgently)* Don't cry. It's good to be awake. Smile, smile for L J. There you go.

*(Enter JACKIE with a box of trophies.)*

JACKIE: I got the rest.

KAREN: What rest? Mel took them all.

JACKIE: He didn't take my ones, or your ones. And this was in Daddy's dresser.

L J: *(To JACKIE)* Stay out of my stuff.

JACKIE: I'm helping.

L J: You pack your things. Leave mine and your Mommy's alone.

KAREN: What one is that?

JACKIE: "Lewis 'the Assassin' Freeman. M V P Roosevelt High School."

KAREN: How come I've never seen it?

L J: It's high school.

KAREN: Someone will buy it. We'll call Uncle Mel.

L J: It's not for sale.

KAREN: Everything is for sale.

L J: Your ring.

KAREN: What about it?

L J: I don't see it on the chopping block.

KAREN: And you won't.

L J: (Looks at his ring) Maybe I should sell this.

KAREN: No.

L J: Why not? You think it's gaudy.

KAREN: We will not sell your Super Bowl ring. It's not even allowed.

JACKIE: Your shit is selling like hotcakes.

KAREN: Young lady, you will not use that language in my house.

JACKIE: Ain't your house. It's for sale.

KAREN: L J—

L J: (Same time) Don't talk back to your Mama.

JACKIE: Ariel asked me could she have something.

KAREN: What?

JACKIE: A t-shirt. Underpants.

KAREN: Jackie!

JACKIE: I didn't sell her any, but you wouldn't miss one. We can sell my school trophies. *(Pulls one from her box)*

L J: We aren't selling your trophies.

JACKIE: Why not? I'm your daughter, I'm famous. And someday I might be a football star, too.

KAREN: Put them with the boxes we're taking to Grandma's.

JACKIE: We can sell Mommy's beauty queen ones. *(Another from her box)*

KAREN: Mine aren't worth anything. Put it back.

L J: I don't know. They might be worth something. We'll ask "Uncle Mel".

JACKIE: Here's Miss Alabama.

L J: Miss Bama, as I live and breathe.

JACKIE: But that's not why you liked her.

L J: Well. It didn't hurt. Everybody likes to look at a pretty girl.

JACKIE: *(Adamant)* You liked her because she was nice and you noticed that.

L J: No, I didn't.

JACKIE: Yes. That's why you brought her food. Because she was a starving mouse.

L J: It wasn't quite like that, was it, Karen?

KAREN: That's what I remember.

L J: *(Fake astonishment)* Really?

KAREN: That's how it seemed.

L J: I wasn't looking for a pretty girl.

KAREN: That's what I'm saying.

L J: *(Pointedly)* Nah, it was different than that.

*(There is danger in the room now.)*

JACKIE: What was it?

KAREN: Yes, L J. What was it?

L J: I was a kid. All I knew was football, I didn't know girls. The whole team was hooking up. With college girls. I don't know nothing about college girls. No college girls in the hood. They were all so clean, and smart, and sarcastic. I don't know what to say to a sarcastic college girl. What if I ask and she turns me down? How bad will that look? Then I see this girl-nothing to look at, not that smart, she for sure won't turn me down.

*(Brief pause)*

JACKIE: Who was that?

L J: That was your Mama. That was the future Miss Alabama. The future Mrs Lewis Jackson Freeman.

*(Brief pause)*

KAREN: I think your Daddy is remembering things wrong.

L J: Nah. That's how it was.

JACKIE: But it changed. Mommy got all pretty and everything.

L J: Yeah, it did. It changed. It got so changed. I met her parents, your Alabama gramma and grampa who never see you. Who call me names but take my money.

KAREN: I don't see them. I gave them up for you.

L J: Happy to live in a house I buy them just as long as I don't visit.

KAREN: My parents, my friends, my town.

L J: You're not welcome there. You are Yankee shame.

JACKIE: What's that?

L J: We move into a neighborhood where my friends get stopped by the cops just for visiting.

KAREN: You wanted to move here.

JACKIE: Mommy...

KAREN: Honey, go on now. Go to your room.

L J: Guilty of D W B.

JACKIE: Daddy...

KAREN: Where are they now? Where are all those friends? Mel and Curtis, that's who is here. And you pay them both.

L J: And you. You on the payroll, too?

(JACKIE *whimpers. Her parents look at her.*)

L J: *(Continued)* Stop it. Stop that.

KAREN: Go on, Honey. Go pack up your room. I'll be right there.

(JACKIE *exits.*)

KAREN: Don't take this out on her.

L J: Don't take what out on her?

KAREN: Your moods, your snippiness. Take it out on me. Don't take it out on her. You gonna talk to me, L J? You ever gonna talk to me?

L J: What's there to say?

(L J *exits.* KAREN *picks up LIttle L and exits. Scene 2. Later.* RUBY's *yard.* L J *with a birdbath and shovel, digs. It hurts.* RUBY *enters.*)

RUBY: Lewis, don't you tear up my habitat.

L J: I'm putting in the birdbath!

RUBY: What does slamming the ground have to do with a birdbath?

L J: I'm not slamming, I'm digging.

RUBY: Then where's the hole?

L J: Under there some place.

RUBY: Weapon of mass destruction.

L J: It's a shovel.

RUBY: I'm not talking about the shovel.

L J: Not me, I'm not that.

RUBY: *(She touches a plant.)* You almost killed my little friend here.

L J: I didn't kill nothing!

RUBY: Well, you almost did.

L J: Here, take it, take it.

*(RUBY does.)*

L J: I'm not a weapon, I'm nothing, I can't even dig a hole.

*(Brief pause)*

RUBY: *(About the plant)* This little friend? First saw him last year, then he popped up again after the winter. Imagine that. Survived all that ice and snow, then managed to struggle up to see the sunshine.

L J: Looks like a weed.

RUBY: A weed that attracts the butterflies and the humming birds. *(Brief pause)* What are you talking about, "You're nothing?" You're my son for one. A husband, for two. Didn't you promise you were going to be a good daddy? Enough things right there to fill up a day...I don't need this bird bath.

L J: Jackie wants it. Only thing she wants from the house.

RUBY: No cause to be mad at her for that.

L J: I'm not mad at Jackie.

RUBY: That's good. Those angry minutes, you don't get them back. Spend a lifetime trying to make up for it.

L J: ...Who you been talking to?

RUBY: Just like always, nobody. You mad about the Roger Daddies?

L J: I don't know.

RUBY: *(Starts to dig)* All we can do is get on with it, Lewis. Ain't no going back.

L J: What are you doing?

RUBY: If Jackie wants it, I'll put it in.

L J: You can't dig in this ground.

RUBY: I'm not some old lady can't shovel a hole. I did more work in this yard than all them yard men put together.

L J: They're still collecting their checks.

RUBY: That's all right, they need the money. *(Weary)* Ground is a bit dry. Maybe this isn't a good idea. The birds are used to my big pot.

L J: Give me the shovel. The birdbath has a ledge so they can stand and shake off the water. They can't do that on your pot rim.

RUBY: What am I supposed to do with my pot?

L J: Make spaghetti. Like the old days. Jackie likes your spaghetti.

RUBY: I'm getting ready to turn the cooking over to Karen. I'm practicing up on my mother-in-law criticisms for her.

L J: You don't have those.

RUBY: Yes, I do. Nobody knows more than me about raising a little Lewis Jackson Freeman—

L J: Oh, God—

RUBY: Baby, Baby, what is it? *(He is silent.)* All we can do is keep going. A little bit at a time. We'll plant this birdbath.

L J: Okay, okay. *(breath)* Your T V still off, Mama?

RUBY: I don't even know where it is.

*(L J exits. RUBY exits. Scene 3. MEL's place. Day six. MEL and KAREN.)*

KAREN: You can't hold the world at bay. The world has a thousand ways of breaking and entering. Might as well open the door and let it all in, let them all in. Take it all away. You can't protect it, might as well just give it away. What's the point of having a house if it can't protect you from the world—I dropped my daughter off at her grandmother's—told her to pick out her room. A room in her loopy grandmother's house, God—

MEL: I need you to talk to L J—

KAREN: *(A laugh)* "What did you expect, what did you expect?" This from my sister who hit on him at our wedding, she doesn't know I know, she told him it was a test. "Oh you passed the test, L J, now I'll let you marry my little sister." You don't expect when you're in love, you're just in love. I was young and stupid and in love, and the disappointments, they are so small and insignificant that you don't want to bring them up because you don't want to upset him, but then they accumulate like a snowball, like an avalanche, and pretty soon, really soon, you're just choking, choking on your own disappointment and your own pettiness, and you can't even see, you can't see what you were thinking when you got married, you have no idea what you *expected*. I've been so silent. *(Realizes)* He's been silent. Maybe he is full of disappointment, too.

MEL: *(Cold)* I don't know. I wasn't there.

KAREN: ...What do you want? Why did I have to come by?

MEL: You should wait on selling the house. He's moving too fast.

KAREN: You want to talk about money? Money?

MEL: You made it clear you're staying with L J, I should back off. Be his friend, you said, don't tell him, you said. You want something else from me, all you have to do is ask.

KAREN: No, I don't want you, Mel, I came to turn you down again. I just thought you'd fight harder for me.

MEL: I'm sorry I disappointed you—

KAREN: What do you want me to do with the house?

MEL: Don't sell it.

KAREN: You're the one screaming about cash. You're the one sold all his trophies on the internet.

MEL: We need the cash. But the house, you're gonna take a hit. Wait until he gives the speech. It's good, it might turn things around.

KAREN: He won't let me see it.

MEL: It's dripping with sincerity—how he loves his fans, how he came up from nothin'. It'll work. Everybody is looking for an excuse to forgive him.

KAREN: L J won't beg.

MEL: He doesn't have to. The circus has moved on.... A governor doing his butler is much more fascinating than your husband hanging a dog.

KAREN: So, Mel, why do we need cash? Why did we have to sell L J's trophies? Lawyer expenses?

MEL: I have a lot of overhead.

KAREN: Making a little nest egg for yourself?

MEL: I have sacrificed for L J—I have forgone other clients to focus on his needs. He has a very complicated balance sheet that includes your parents, your sister, many friends, and his mother. Not to mention private school and charities.

KAREN: You need to get some other clients.

MEL: And I will.

KAREN: And you should stay away from their wives.

MEL: ...I don't go after wives. You were never L J's wife. You were always Karen to me. Just say the word. I'm ready to give it all up. Just say the word.

KAREN: Stop it. You're relieved. If he's not going to lose his job, you want it all to go back the way it was.

MEL: We have a son—

KAREN: L J has a son.

MEL: Technically.

KAREN: And legally and– *(fumbling, desperate)* and all other ways.

*(KAREN exits. MEL exits. Meanwhile. Scene 4. RUBY's. JACKIE and RUBY look at a room from the doorway. They hold hands.)*

RUBY: This bedroom doesn't look so good now, but I'll get it cleaned up for you.

JACKIE: *(Appalled)* I never seen anything like this in my whole life. What happened in here?

RUBY: *(Entering the room)* I left the windows open so the animals could get out of the snow. But don't worry, I closed off the vents so I didn't waste the heat.

JACKIE: *(Following)* It smells.

RUBY: Raccoon poop.

JACKIE: Raccoons did this?

RUBY: Mostly. Squirrels. Birds. I was hoping for a deer, but the gates keep them out.

JACKIE: *(An order)* You can't let wild animals in your house.

RUBY: They're good company scurrying around at night. Like a party.

JACKIE: You could get rats.

RUBY: The rats live under the porch.

JACKIE: This is not sanitary.

RUBY: Raccoons wash their food and they clean their fur. And they like the dark. I like an animal likes the dark, lives in the dark part of the day.

JACKIE: Nocturnal.

RUBY: What's that?

JACKIE: That's what it's called. When you like the night.

RUBY: What's it called when you like the day?

JACKIE: Normal.

RUBY: Then I guess I'm normal.

JACKIE: No, Gramma. I don't want to sleep with raccoons.

RUBY: Your Daddy is always trying to hire me help. We'll hire us a guy with a shovel.

JACKIE: We can't hire people. We're poor.

RUBY: Well...I can still sweep and shovel with the best of them. And your Daddy can help.

JACKIE: Daddy don't bend anymore. He can't catch me. He got stuck. Like an old man.

RUBY: I don't like to hear about that.

JACKIE: You seen Little L yet, Gramma?

RUBY: I have not had the pleasure, but I'm ready and eager. Soon as your Mama feels the time is right.

JACKIE: He's white.

RUBY: You were a light baby.

JACKIE: He's whiter than me.

RUBY: Well. Makes it easier to see the dirt.

JACKIE: Where's he going to sleep?

RUBY: You want him in with you?

JACKIE: I do not. He's a responsibility.

RUBY: He can stay with your Mama and Daddy. Or with me. Or the den. The basement. The attic—the living room—the family room—one of the seven walk-in closets—the pantry—the kitchen—the game room. I know—! He can rent the servant's quarters over the garage.

(JACKIE *and* RUBY *laugh.*)

RUBY: Your Daddy and me lived in an apartment smaller than this room for eleven years and we never called it crowded.

JACKIE: No. You lived with your parents.

RUBY: We lived with my parents until they died, then we got our own place. Lewis slept in a bedroom smaller than any of these closets. I slept on the sofa. Not even a sofa bed. Just a lumpy two-seater couch. Cooked in the same room as the T V. Still had Christmas dinners for twelve.

JACKIE: Who came? You don't have any family.

RUBY: Strays. Lewis's friends from school. They would all bring me presents, cards they made with school supplies, drawings.... The dinners stopped after he got to high school. He had different friends once he started playing ball.

JACKIE: I don't much like Little L.

RUBY: I suspect he'll grow on you over time.

JACKIE: It was better before he came. He's why Daddy's so sad.

RUBY: A child is no reason for anybody to be sad. We rejoice in our children.

JACKIE: Are you allowed to send children back?

RUBY: With children, there is no back. We have our children until we die. Or until they do.

*(Meanwhile. Scene 5. Press Conference. L J walks to a podium. He has no pieces of paper. Flashbulbs and cameras. At their homes, MEL, KAREN, and MRS JONES watch on their respective T Vs. A moment of silence, then it comes out in a slow steady flood.)*

L J: I loved that dog—sweet dog, good girl—wasn't her fault, she was kissing me, and I was, I don't even know, a monster, I was a monster, I saw it, I saw what you saw and I screamed, I screamed when I saw it, who is that? That ain't me, that can't be me, who acts like that, who does that, not a man, not a Daddy, but wasn't nobody there but me, can't blame, can't blame somebody wasn't there, it was me, oh, my god, it was me. I want to go back, I want to go back and make it go away, but I can't go back, there's no going back. If I could disappear, I would disappear, take all the hurt away, bring back that sweet dog. All I want to do is disappear.

*(L J exits, as do KAREN, MEL, and MRS JONES. Later. Scene 6. RUBY's. JACKIE, RUBY, and now MRS JONES.)*

MRS JONES: I wasn't sure you'd remember me.

RUBY: I remember you. I still have your book.

MRS JONES: What book?

RUBY: *Animals of Australia.*

MRS JONES: ...Was that? ...Oh. Okay.

RUBY: That book changed my life. I cried when Lewis tried to take it back to the library. Say, Hi, to Mrs. Jones, Jackie. She's your Daddy's science teacher.

JACKIE: I'm fourth grade.

MRS JONES: Your Daddy says you're very smart.

JACKIE: I'm average smart. But I'm very fast and good at sports. You want to see?

MRS JONES: I do.

JACKIE: *(She is the quarterback lined up behind an imaginary center.)* Hut one, hut two. *(Takes the imaginary ball, falls back, and throws.)* Touchdown, touchdown.

MRS JONES: You look just like Lewis.

JACKIE: Really? Mommy says I look like her northern Italian ancestors.

MRS JONES: Not when you play football.

JACKIE: She says girls aren't allowed to play.

MRS JONES: Maybe they'll change the rules for you.

JACKIE: *(Happy at that)* I think they will. Would you like me to get you something, Mrs Jones?

MRS JONES: No thank you, I'm fine.

JACKIE: Good. We're living off the land.

MRS JONES: *(To RUBY)* I was...worried about Lewis. I didn't want to go to the house, and I can't get through on the phone.

JACKIE: We're unlisted.

MRS JONES: I have the number.

JACKIE: Then he don't want to talk to you. We have caller I D. Ariel and Lisa do that, too. They don't want to talk to somebody they let it go to voicemail. I always answer.

RUBY: *(Trying to remember something)* The koala bear?

MRS JONES: Yes?

RUBY: The cute little guy that has claws this long?

MRS JONES: Yes, they can be vicious—

RUBY: I know, I read the book. What's it called? *(Gestures to her stomach)* Kangaroos?

MRS JONES: ...Marsupial?

RUBY: Yes! Marsupial. It would have been nice, a little pouch like that, to protect Lewis from the world.

MRS JONES: He's so sad.

JACKIE: Daddy's not sad.

MRS JONES: At the press conference, on T V—

JACKIE: *(Pointedly and slowly, to let MRS JONES know RUBY doesn't know.)* We don't watch T V. We pulled the wires. We don't watch YouTube. We don't watch anything in this house. Okay?!

MRS JONES: *(Realizing)* Oh. Well. Good. That's good. I should probably—

JACKIE: Daddy's going to be alright. He has too many responsibilities, that's all.

RUBY: I'm getting his room ready.

*(They exit. Scene 7. Day nine. L J's house. L J surrounded by packing boxes. MEL enters.)*

MEL: Why haven't you answered the phone? It's been three days.

L J: Took a page out of Ruby's playbook. I pulled all the wires.

MEL: I emailed.

L J: Phone, internet, T V, radio. All the wires are pulled.

MEL: I was so pissed—I worked hard on that speech.
But...what you said worked. Everybody thought it was
a suicide note.

L J: I don't know what I said.

MEL: You can watch it online. Didn't I tell you? Give
it a little time? Time—the great American healer. You
might still have to go to court, but Champion wants
you at camp—

L J: How's *his* back?

MEL: ...Something wrong with his back?

L J: Listen to him, "We took some hits out there, we
made some mistakes, but we're looking to improve—
we'll be back strong next Sunday." Sounds like he's the
player gonna spend the week with ice bags taped to his
shoulder.

MEL: ...Um. He's the one called me—told me to get
over here. The whole world is now worried about L J
Freeman. I love America.

L J: *(But he means it.)* I do, too.

MEL: Rico called. He's not filing charges. You were
great, L J.

L J: I gave him the truck.

MEL: You what?

L J: It wasn't the speech. I asked him what I could do to
make up for his dog. He said he wanted my truck.

MEL: Oh. Well. Um. At least you don't have to sell
the house. You need help putting stuff back? I can get
some people over here.

L J: It's fine.

MEL: I took the trophies off eBay, but some of them
were gone already. I'll try to get them back.

L J: I don't need them back.

MEL: Okay. Don't worry it's all going to be fine.

L J: I don't have to become a Curtis?

MEL: A what?

L J: A houseboy for another N F L guy?

MEL: You do not.

L J: Curtis, he gets a call, a survey, they want to know if he has experienced any signs of dementia. "Nah, he says, I don't get those."

MEL: Curtis took a lot of hits to the head.

L J: Yeah, he did. Curtis can't remember where he parked the truck, but I always had enough time to complete a pass.

MEL: That's the game.

L J: Oh, yeah. That's why they pay us.

MEL: *(Brief pause)* You're ready, aren't you? For camp?

L J: What about their morals clause? They're going to, what? Un-invoke it?

MEL: They're going to pretend it was all a bad dream.

*(L J is calm and in control, still messin' with* MEL.*)*

L J: ...I've been having a little shoulder pain.

MEL: What pain? What shoulder pain?

L J: An injury I got season before last.

MEL: What injury—who knows about it?

L J: Me. Doctor on the east side. You.

MEL: *(Making sure)* You didn't go to the team doctor?

L J: I wasn't quite ready to say goodbye to the game.

MEL: Okay. Here's how we play it. You go back to work, you go to camp, you get the injury in camp—

L J: But that's a lie—

MEL: L J. You will get this injury after you are reinstated, during training camp. Thus ensuring your full salary for this year.

L J: ...Maybe that's a good idea. All them millions. Put some away for a change.

MEL: You bet it's a good idea.

L J: What's our contract say?

MEL: Which contract?

L J: Yours and mine.

MEL: ...About what?

L J: You still my lawyer if I don't play?

MEL: Why wouldn't you play? You get reinstated, you get your salary, you take off the year, get some surgery, you're back in the game.

L J: I'm just curious is all.

MEL: I'm still your lawyer if you play or don't.

L J: Can I afford you if I don't?

MEL: My salary comes out of your salary. Eighteen percent of your salary is what I get paid.

L J: So the money from the trophies, that's all mine?

MEL: I get a percentage of merchandizing and endorsements.

L J: My old trophies are merchandizing?

MEL: ...You could probably challenge that.

L J: But then I'd need a lawyer.

MEL: That is true.

L J: How long you figure you can stay afloat if I don't play?

MEL: Twelve weeks.

L J: About the same as us.

MEL: Why wouldn't you play?

(KAREN *enters with Little L.*)

MEL: Who have we here? Hello, Little Man, Little Mother.

KAREN: He just woke up.

MEL: Can I hold him?

L J: (*Taking Little L from* KAREN) Nope. His Daddy is going to hold him. Hello Lewis Jackson Freeman, Junior. How's it hanging, pal. Yeah, that's funny. Your Daddy is a funny man.

MEL: Well....

KAREN: Goodbye, Mel.

MEL: I'll leave you to it. (*He exits.*)

L J: (*In pain*) "Little Mother" Take him—take him—

KAREN: Here... (*Taking back the baby, putting him down.*) L J, what's wrong?

(L J *shakes his head.*)

KAREN: What is it?

L J: Oh, man...

KAREN: Sit down. Where does it hurt.

L J: Neck. Shoulder. Elbow. Back.

KAREN: Let me... (*She massages* L J's *neck and arm. Some silence*) Might have started out like that.

L J: What? What you talking about?

KAREN: Started out I was the mouse who for sure wouldn't turn you down.

L J: Oh. Yeah, it did.

KAREN: All my girlfriends, "Oh my god, L J Freeman, Karen, you are the luckiest girl I know." Then you took me out again. And again. But you were quiet and I

talked too much, and we didn't even kiss goodnight.
You were shy, and I was bored. I didn't let on that L J
Freeman was a dud.

*(L J laughs, KAREN is encouraged.)*

KAREN: Might be a fine player of football, but the
man is a dud on a date. All those girls hanging on my
every word, I started to make stuff up. I lied and said
you took me in your arms ever so gently touched my
mouth with yours, and ever so gently touched my
breast. I said my dream for how I wanted you to be.
And once I said it, I knew that's how it should be, and
I led you to me, and once you found me, you took the
reins right out of my hand, and touched me like no boy
ever had before, and kissed me, and loved me. I mighta
started out as a mouse but you came to love me, and
I was amazed that it could be possible, and I made
myself lovely because you deserved it.

L J: *(Brief pause)* ...And now...what? I stopped deserving
it? Somebody else started deserving it?

*(Pause, it's out now.)*

KAREN: I—I—...You wouldn't talk to me. I couldn't get
through to you. It was months, L J.

L J: *(He stands.)* And you run to "Uncle Mel"?

KAREN: *(She stands.)* It was a mistake—it was over
before it started—

L J: *(Mocking)* Yeah, not quite. Why did you have that
baby? Did you think it was mine?

KAREN: I couldn't—

L J: Why did you name him after me?

KAREN: I thought—

L J: You thought you'd have another "light" baby,
nobody would know? Maybe *your* people don't know
the difference. *My* people know.

KAREN: I thought...I couldn't stand you feeling sorry for me, that's what I thought. Oh sure, run to a doctor, make it go away, tell you I had a miscarriage, and you would feel so sorry for me. I couldn't let you feel sorry for me.

L J: Well you get what you want. I don't feel sorry for you.

KAREN: Did you have a girlfriend? Is that why you didn't want me anymore?

L J: No.

KAREN: All those pretty girls all the time, I felt like such a mouse—

L J: No.

KAREN: I'm sorry, I'm so sorry—

L J: It's all going to be alright. The money and everything.

KAREN: I don't care about money—

L J: Yeah, you do, you like all that, and our Uncle Mel has it all figured—I go to training camp- get this shoulder injury—collect my eight million dollars—

KAREN: Please, Baby—

L J: But you and Jackie and your son, y'all gotta go. You can move in with Mama. It'll be good for her. I need some space.

KAREN: *(Desperate)* For better or worse- 'til death do us part.

L J: The dog's dead. Does that count?

*(L J exits. KAREN exits. JACKIE enters and stands over and looks into Little L's carrier. She stays there for Scene 8. RUBY's. A few days later; Day twelve. RUBY takes JACKIE's hand as the two of them look into Little L's carrier.)*

JACKIE: White, ain't he?

RUBY: *(She knows.)* Light, he's very light.

JACKIE: What do you see, Gramma, what do you see?!

RUBY: I see...your brother. I see a beautiful baby looks just like his sister.

JACKIE: He don't look nothing like me.

RUBY: When you were a puppy you looked like this boy in this basket.

JACKIE: Why can't I go live with Daddy in our house?

RUBY: You barely been here. Give it some time.

JACKIE: Will Daddy visit me?

RUBY: Of course he will. He can't stay away from you and my sweet little grandson.

JACKIE: Don't you start liking him, Gramma.

RUBY: It's too late. I am full up with this boy. Want to put him in my little mommy pouch, run off with him.

JACKIE: Good. You and Little L run off, leave the rest of us here. Let Mommy get the smell out of the house. She's a whiz with Lysol.

RUBY: I don't allow Lysol. It is poison on the water.

JACKIE: She sneaked it in. In her pouch.

RUBY: I must stop her cleaning frenzy.

JACKIE: She's upstairs in the back.

RUBY: Cleaning is very bad for the planet.

*(RUBY exits. JACKIE makes sure she has gone. Turns to face the baby, crosses and stands over him. Takes the choke collar from her pocket, holds it over her head in a fury and snarls at the baby, the same way she snarled in imitation of L J hanging the dog. L J has witnessed her behavior.)*

L J: No.

*(JACKIE whirls around on him, still snarling loudly.)*

L J: *(Enveloping her, taking the collar)* Baby, no. no.

JACKIE: "Get off me!"

L J: Jackie—Baby—

JACKIE: I could read your lips, you said "Get off me, off me!"

L J: I got you. It's okay.

JACKIE: You hate him.

L J: I don't hate him. Nobody hates a little baby.

JACKIE: He's why you sent us away.

L J: Ain't his fault—

JACKIE: You sent us away—

L J: I got you now, not letting you go now.

JACKIE: I'm like you, Daddy, I'm just like you.

L J: You are. You're just like me— *(Noticing the crying baby)* Look what we did. Made him all scared of the world. We're supposed to protect him. Stand between him and all the dangers. That's what Daddies do.

JACKIE: He's too much—he's too much.

L J: Baby, baby, baby. Ain't no going back. Can't undo the bad; can't undo the good.

JACKIE: I can undo him.

L J: He's your brother. You gotta let him into your heart. Once you let him in, there's no going back.

JACKIE: I don't know how to do that.

L J: I held his whole self in my hand and I made a promise, I am your Daddy for now and forever and I will not let you down. Just like I made to you.

JACKIE: I don't remember a promise.

L J: I held you and I held your Mama's hand. It was the best moment of my life.

JACKIE: I want to hear my promise.

L J: *(A forever promise)* I am your Daddy for now and forever and I will never let you down.

*(Brief pause)*

JACKIE: Okay.

L J: Unless you hurt your brother, and then you're outta here on your butt.

*(L J hugs JACKIE.)*

JACKIE: Let me go, Daddy.

L J: Nuh uh. Not ever.

JACKIE: I'm not going to hurt him. I want to pick him up. Mommy won't let me.

L J: She just scared you'll drop him. You know how she gets.

*(L J sits JACKIE down and places the baby in her arms.)*

JACKIE: He don't weigh nothing.

L J: You didn't weigh nothing neither.

JACKIE: Who does he look like?

L J: ...You. That's what you looked like. But you was rounder. Butter ball.

JACKIE: He's really soft.

L J: Yeah.

*(JACKIE starts to fall apart.)*

JACKIE: So I have to be really careful.

L J: You do. The soft ones break.

JACKIE: That's why Mommy wouldn't let me...I wasn't gonna...I wasn't gonna...I wasn't—

L J: I know, Baby, I know. It's okay. Nobody's gonna— ever again. It's okay. Let him in, he wants to come in. Let him wash you all over in his love.

JACKIE: *(Crying)* I think he's peeing on me.

L J: That ain't pee. That is the warmth of his whole love. Look at that little smile.

JACKIE: That's his peeing smile.

*(RUBY and KAREN enter unseen by L J and JACKIE.)*

L J: He's not scared now. Now his big sister has a hold of him.

JACKIE: I am your big sister, now and forever, and I will never let you down. Don't worry about how white you are. It's easier to see the dirt on a white child.

L J: Ain't gonna be any dirt with your Mama around to wipe him off. He'll be lucky if she lets him play outside before he's eighteen.

JACKIE: We'll tell Mommy he's running track, but really he can be at football practice.

L J: Why didn't I ever think of that?

RUBY: You did.

*(L J and JACKIE see KAREN and RUBY.)*

L J: Right. I did think of it, didn't I. *(Brief pause)* Hey, Karen.

KAREN: Hey.

L J: Me and Curtis brought over some of your boxes. He's in the back looking at Mama's birds.

RUBY: Give me my grandbaby, Jackie. *(Takes him)*

JACKIE: Don't drop him.

RUBY: I don't drop babies. Let's you and me show him our habitat.

*(JACKIE and RUBY and Little L exit.)*

L J: Whachu got there?

KAREN: Vinegar. Ruby hid my Lysol.

L J: How's the cleanup going?

KAREN: Slow. Lysol is faster.

L J: You got room over here for me and Curtis?

KAREN: We got enough room...for the Army. But I thought—

L J: Change of plans.

KAREN: Since when?

L J: Since now.

(L J *opens his hand; the choke collar falls open and then he lets it fall to the floor. When it is silent:*)

L J: *(Continued)* She's just like me.

KAREN: She wants to be.

L J: I gotta give up the game. Right now, today—it's over. I can't go back—

KAREN: You don't have to go back for me—

L J: There's not going to be any money—

KAREN: I don't care.

L J: I don't know... *(Brief pause)* Shit.

KAREN: Anything, I'll do anything.

L J: I hold him and we're in here and it's me and Jackie and him and it feels alright, I'm the Daddy, I get to be the Daddy. What about out there? What am I supposed to do when I have to...take him to the playground?

*(Brief pause)*

KAREN: *(Grasping at straws)* We'll get our own swing set. There's room back there.

*(Brief pause during which* KAREN *and* L J *almost laugh, but don't.)*

L J: Come here, Baby.

*(*KAREN *and* L J *embrace for dear life.)*

L J: *(To the sky)* Here we go.
*(They hold on. The end.)*